von Wolfgang Hamm

15-Minuten-Tests
Englisch Klasse 7/8

Ernst Klett Schulbuchverlag
Stuttgart · Leipzig

Inhaltsverzeichnis

Bildquellen: Seite 10: Alamy Images RM (Popperfoto), Abingdon, Oxon; Seite 16: Pixtal, New York, NY; Seite 21: MEV, Augsburg; Seite 24: Corbis (Tim Graham/Sygma), Düsseldorf; Seite 31: Picture-Alliance (KPA/HIP/AnnR), Frankfurt; Seite 38: HIPP-Foto, Berlin; Seite 59: Corbis (C. Felver), Düsseldorf; Seite 66: Picture-Alliance (KPA), Frankfurt; Seite 72: GOODSHOOT (Goodshoot), Annecy-Le-Vieux; Seite 73, Bild 1: Klett-Archiv (Susanne Möhring), Stuttgart; Seite 73, Bild 2: shutterstock (Alan C. Heison), New York, NY

1. Auflage 1 6 5 4 3 2 1 | 2012 2011 2010 2009 2008

Alle Drucke dieser Auflage sind unverändert und können im Unterricht nebeneinander verwendet werden.
Die letzte Zahl bezeichnet das Jahr des Druckes.

Internetadresse: www.klett.de

Autor: Wolfgang Hamm, Marktredwitz
Redaktion: Birgit Piefke-Wagner, Korntal-Münchingen

Layoutkonzeption und Satz: Susanne Möhring
Umschlaggestaltung: Susanne Möhring
Titelbild: shutterstock (RF/JoLin), New York
Reproduktion: Meyle + Müller, Medien-Management, Pforzheim
Druck: Druckhaus Götz GmbH, Ludwigsburg

Printed in Germany
ISBN 978-3-12-582658-8

9 783125 826588

Liebe Schülerin, lieber Schüler,

jeder der 15-Minuten Tests besteht aus 35 Fragen mit vier möglichen Antworten. Die Antworten müssen nur angekreuzt werden. Es gibt jeweils nur eine richtige Lösung. Die Aufgabenstellung ist absichtlich unterschiedlich gestellt, so dass du manchmal das Richtige, manchmal aber auch das Falsche von den vier Möglichkeiten herausfinden musst. Daher solltest du die Arbeitsanweisungen ganz genau lesen!

Diese Tests sind für 7. und 8. Klassen aller Schularten gedacht. Sie können zu Hause als unterhaltsame Erweiterung deiner sprachlichen Fähigkeiten eingesetzt werden, als Übungsmaterial zur Gewöhnung an zunehmend standardisierte Testformen, zur Abwechslung im Schulalltag, um Zwischenbilanz zu ziehen.
Für jeden Test sollten etwa 15 Minuten eingeplant werden. Diese Testform wird zunehmend in der Schule und bei Bewerbungen eingesetzt. Auch dort hast du für die Bearbeitung nur begrenzt Zeit. Halte dich daher nicht zu lange an Aufgaben auf, die du nicht auf Anhieb verstehst. Hab' auch Mut, Lösungen zu erraten.
Wer nichts ankreuzt, bekommt auf jeden Fall keinen Punkt.
Die Tests folgen einer Progression, d. h. die leichteren Tests stehen am Anfang und werden nach hinten immer ein bisschen schwieriger.

Deinen bearbeiteten Test kannst du selbst kontrollieren, indem du im Lösungsteil die richtigen Antworten mit deinen Antworten vergleichst. Im Lösungsteil erhältst du auch interessante Zusatzinformationen zu einigen Aufgaben. Am Ende des Buches kannst du die erreichte Punktzahl in eine Tabelle eintragen und hast so einen Überblick über deinen Lernerfolg.
Mit jedem Test wird *Learning by testing* praktiziert, d. h. die konzentrierte Durchführung der Tests mit ihren unterschiedlichen Fragestellungen schulen dein Sprachverständnis und erweitern deine Kenntnisse im Englischen in so wichtigen Bereichen wie Vokabular, Grammatik, Leseverstehen, Kommunikation, Landeskunde, Aussprache und Rechtschreibung.
Das sollte dir eine Viertelstunde wert sein! Viel Spaß beim Testen.

Los geht's mit Test 1!

Vocabulary

1 **Which one is never made of *leather*?**

a) a handbag ☐
b) a purse ☐
c) a bucket ☐
d) trousers ☐

2 **Which of these is never *black*?**

a) coal ☐
b) tree ☐
c) cat ☐
d) hair ☐

3 **Find the odd one.**

a) break ☐
b) breakfast ☐
c) lunch ☐
d) dinner ☐

4 **You switch it on at night when you want to read a book.**

a) an alarm clock ☐
b) a calculator ☐
c) a light ☐
d) a toaster ☐

5 **Three in one. Which word describes all the other three?**

a) tea ☐
b) coffee ☐
c) drink ☐
d) hot chocolate ☐

6 **British English (BE) and American English (AE): Which pair isn't correct?**

a) BE: form – AE: grade ☐
b) BE: timetable – AE: schedule ☐
c) BE: mark – AE: note ☐
d) BE: pupil – AE: student ☐

7 **Which word is wrong?**

a) four ☐
b) fourteen ☐
c) fourty ☐
d) forty-four ☐

8 ***A mother's girl is her …***

a) grandchild. ☐
b) daughter. ☐
c) niece. ☐
d) cousin. ☐

9 **Kate war letzte Woche zum *Casting*, d.h. Sie war zum … eingeladen.**

a) Vorstellungsgespräch ☐
b) Vorentscheid ☐
c) Vorsprechen und Vorsingen ☐
d) Vorbereitungstraining ☐

Language

10 **Which word is not pronounced with [iː]?**

a) dream ☐
b) steak ☐
c) key ☐
c) feel ☐

11 **Which word has no [ɔ:] ?**

a) hour ☐
b) four ☐
c) your ☐
d) more ☐

12 **What does *a.m.* not mean?**

a) before noon ☐
b) American ☐
c) in the morning ☐
d) before midday ☐

13 **Complete this proverb.**

You can't teach an old … new tricks.
a) dog ☐
b) horse ☐
c) cat ☐
d) monkey ☐

14 **Complete this proverb.**

Better late than …
a) no one. ☐
b) never. ☐
c) nothing. ☐
d) not. ☐

Reading

15 **Where can you read this sign?**

SLOW DOWN – CHILDREN CROSSING

a) on the motorway ☐
b) in the park ☐
c) outside a school ☐
d) inside a school ☐

16 **Read this ad. Which sentence ending is correct?**

You don't have to pay for …

a) the cats. ☐
b) the dogs. ☐
c) the children. ☐
d) phone call. ☐

FREE KITTENS TO GOOD HOME.

Ten weeks old, very playful. Two females and one male. Grey and white kittens. Good with dogs and children. They must go before our baby comes. Please call after 5 p.m. (01603-79 84 21) or e-mail me at suebrown@x-line.uk

17 **What information can you get from this ad?**

Sue Brown wants to …

a) have a new kitchen. ☐
b) buy a dog. ☐
c) find a new home for three kittens. ☐
d) find a new home for the baby. ☐

18 **What does this notice mean?**

There will be a disco …

a) on Friday. ☐
b) this week. ☐
c) on Thursday next week. ☐
d) outside the gym. ☐

Communication

19 **Which verb is correct in this question?**

Could you … me the way to the station, please?

a) explain ☐
b) say ☐
c) inform ☐
d) tell ☐

20 ***You want to say hello.* What can you not say?**

a) Good morning/afternoon/evening. ☐
b) How do you do? ☐
c) Fine, thanks. ☐
d) Pleased to meet you. ☐

21 **What's the best answer to this question:**

Can I use your MP3 player?

a) What a pity. ☐
b) Yes, I don't mind. ☐
c) Excuse me, please. ☐
d) No, of course. ☐

22 **Which of these sentences can you write to *finish* a letter?**

a) What a surprise to get a postcard from you. ☐
b) Thank you very much for your interesting letter. ☐
c) Give my regards to your parents. ☐
d) I enjoyed reading your last e-mail. ☐

Grammar

23 **One form is wrong.**

a) fall – fell – fallen ☐
b) eat – ate – eaten ☐
c) drive – drove – driven ☐
d) break – broke – breaken ☐

24 **Which article isn't correct?**

a) an exercise book ☐
b) a German song ☐
c) an uniform ☐
d) an English song ☐

25 **Which plural is wrong?**

a) two women ☐
b) three children ☐
c) four peoples ☐
d) five men ☐

26 Choose the correct pronoun.

While we were working with saws and hammers, we hurt …

a) us. ☐
b) our. ☐
c) ours. ☐
d) ourselves. ☐

27 Which ending of the sentence isn't correct?

I was in London …

a) two months ago. ☐
b) last year. ☐
c) for two years. ☐
d) before one year. ☐

28 Find the wrong s-genitive.

a) Nina's CD player ☐
b) Charles's friends ☐
c) the children's toys ☐
d) the Brown's house ☐

29 Which ending is correct?

Kate has to go to the …

a) doctors next week. ☐
b) doctor's next week. ☐
c) doctors's next week. ☐
d) doctor next week. ☐

Culture

30 Who was it?

a) The Sheriff of Nottingham ☐
b) Little John ☐
c) Robin Hood ☐
d) Friar Tuck ☐

This man lived in a forest in England more than 500 years ago. He and his friends stole money from the rich and gave it to the poor.

31 **Read the text again and find the wrong statement.**

a) Rich people helped the poor. ☐
b) The legend is more than 500 years old. ☐
c) He and his friends took money from the rich. ☐
d) He and his friends were criminals. ☐

32 ***You can see the famous statue of this man in …***

a) Manchester. ☐
b) Glasgow. ☐
c) Dover. ☐
d) Nottingham. ☐

33 **Which country is not part of Great Britain?**

a) England ☐
b) Scotland ☐
c) Wales ☐
d) Ireland ☐

34 **Mark the wrong capital.**

a) England – London ☐
b) Scotland – Glasgow ☐
c) Wales – Cardiff ☐
d) Northern Ireland – Belfast ☐

Extra tip

35 **Welcher Tipp ist überflüssig?**

Beim Englischlernen zu Hause ist es wichtig, dass …
a) es im Zimmer immer angenehm warm/kühl ist. ☐
b) ich immer gutes Licht (Fenster, Lampe) habe. ☐
c) der Schreibtisch jeden Tag von meinen Eltern aufgeräumt wird. ☐
d) meine Schreibsachen, Bücher und Hefte immer griffbereit sind. ☐

Vocabulary

1 Which one is usually not made of *glass*?

a) a mirror ☐
b) a screen ☐
c) a phone ☐
d) a bottle ☐

2 Which of these isn't *white*?

a) clouds ☐
b) sky ☐
c) snow ☐
d) salt ☐

3 Find the odd one.

a) eye ☐
b) saw ☐
c) ear ☐
d) nose ☐

4 Where do you go if you want to borrow books?

a) booking office ☐
b) station ☐
c) library ☐
d) bookshop ☐

5 Three in one. Which word describes all the other three?

a) desk ☐
b) armchair ☐
c) cupboard ☐
d) furniture ☐

6 **British English (BE) and American English (AE): Which pair isn't correct?**

a) BE: theatre – AE: theater ☐
b) BE: ground floor – AE: first floor ☐
c) BE: flat – AE: living room ☐
d) BE: toilet – AE: bathroom ☐

7 **Which written number is wrong?**

a) £150 → one hundred and fifty pounds ☐
b) 1,550 miles → one thousand five hundred and fifty-five miles ☐
c) in 1995 → in nineteen ninety-five ☐
d) $25,000 → twenty-five thousand dollars ☐

8 ***A father's boy is his …***

a) grandchild. ☐
b) cousin. ☐
c) son. ☐
d) nephew. ☐

9 **Kate benutzt in letzter Zeit gerne *Make-up*, d.h. …**

a) Schminke ☐
b) Maske ☐
c) Lippenstift ☐
d) Gel ☐

Language

10 **Which word has no [u:]?**

a) food ☐
b) foot ☐
c) school ☐
d) tool ☐

11 **Which word has no [ʌ] ?**

a) put ☐
b) cut ☐
c) sun ☐
d) but ☐

12 **What does *p.m.* not mean?**

a) after noon ☐
b) popular man ☐
c) in the evening ☐
d) after midday ☐

13 **Complete this proverb.**

The early bird …

a) sings a song. ☐
b) brings a baby. ☐
c) wakes the farmer. ☐
d) catches the worm. ☐

14 **Complete this proverb.**

A bird in the hand is worth …

a) a nest in the tree. ☐
b) two (birds) in the bush. ☐
c) three goldfish in a tank. ☐
d) four castles in Scotland. ☐

Reading

15 **Where can you read this sign?**

BED & BREAKFAST

a) In hospital. ☐
b) In a church. ☐
c) In the country. ☐
d) On a ship. ☐

16 **Read this ad and then tick the only correct information.**

a) The Morrisons want to give Leslie some sweets. ☐
b) The Morrisons are going to have a party. ☐
c) Leslie was born 7th July, 1990. ☐
d) Leslie gets a lot of birthday cards. ☐

BIRTHDAYS

Happy 17th Birthday
on 7th July, 2007
Leslie Morrison,
my darling, my sweetheart,
my honey.
Love from Gilbert S.
and your Mum, Dad and Geoff

17 **Read the ad again. Which fact is correct?**

a) Geoff is Leslie's boyfriend. ☐
b) Gilbert is Leslie's boyfriend. ☐
c) Leslie has no friends. ☐
d) Geoff and Gilbert are brothers. ☐

18 **Which sentence is not true?**

a) The longest opening time is on Sundays. ☐
b) On Saturdays you can buy tickets in the afternoon. ☐
c) The counter is open for six hours on Fridays and Saturdays. ☐
d) On Tuesdays you can buy tickets after 5 o'clock. ☐

TICKET OFFICE
CINEMA 2020
OPEN MON TILL THU: 5 P.M.–8 P.M.
FRI AND SAT: 4 P.M.–10 P.M.
SUN: 2 P.M.–8 P.M.

Communication

19 **Which word is correct?**

Excuse me, could you give me a … to the station?

a) trip ☐
b) taxi ☐
c) lift ☐
d) takeaway ☐

20 **Which answer is correct?**

My name's Kate. How do you do? …

a) I'm fine, thank you. ☐
b) Very well, pleasant. ☐
c) It's OK. ☐
d) No problem. ☐

21 Which answer is not correct?

Have a nice holiday. …

a) Thank you. ☐
b) You, too. ☐
c) (The) same to you. ☐
d) All the same. ☐

22 What can you write to *start* a letter?

a) I was glad to get your postcard last Monday. ☐
b) Could you write again, please? ☐
c) Please write soon. ☐
d) I can hardly wait to get your letter. ☐

Grammar

23 Spot the wrong form.

a) teach – taught – taught ☐
b) thing – thought – thought ☐
c) catch – caught – caught ☐
d) buy – bought – bought ☐

24 Finish the sentence.

We live …

a) in the York Road. ☐
b) in York Road. ☐
c) at York Road. ☐
d) on York Road. ☐

25 Which long form isn't correct?

a) *She isn't celebrating* her birthday this year.
= She is not celebrating … ☐
b) *She's* fifteen now. = She is … ☐
c) *She's got* two cats. = She is got … ☐
d) *She's waiting* for her friend, Julia. = She is waiting … ☐

26 **Find the wrong word.**

a) Have you got *any* pears? ☐
b) Sorry, we haven't got *some*. ☐
c) But we've got *some* fresh kiwis today. ☐
d) No, thanks, I've got *some* kiwis at home. ☐

27 **Which sentence isn't correct?**

a) I hope I'll soon get a new mobile. ☐
b) I hope I'll get a new mobile for my next birthday. ☐
c) I hope I got a new mobile for my last birthday. ☐
d) I hope I'll get a new mobile in two months' time. ☐

28 **Which plural form isn't correct?**

a) one tomato – two tomatoes ☐
b) one potato – two potatoes ☐
c) one photo – two photoes ☐
d) one radio – two radios ☐

29 **Which plural form is wrong?**

a) one roof – two rooves ☐
b) one knife – two knives ☐
c) one wife – two wives ☐
d) one shelf – two shelves ☐

Culture

30 **Who was it?**

a) Henry VIII ☐
b) Noel Coward ☐
c) William Shakespeare ☐
d) Bobby Moore ☐

Many people say his works are some of the greatest in English literature. He wrote dozens of wonderful plays for the theatre. They have been famous for more than 400 years. His plays were first shown in the Globe Theatre in London.

31 **Read the text again and find the wrong statement.**

a) People still like him because he wrote a dozen plays for the theatre. ☐
b) Although his plays are more than 400 years old they are still well-known. ☐
c) The Globe Theatre in London performed his plays for the first time. ☐
d) Many people think his plays are the best ever written in the English language. ☐

32 **Which play is not written by him?**

a) Romeo and Julia ☐
b) Macbeth ☐
c) Hamlet ☐
d) Faust ☐

33 **Christmas in Great Britain.**

Who comes through the chimney and brings presents to the children in Great Britain? …

a) An angel. ☐
b) Father Rudolph. ☐
c) A reindeer. ☐
d) Santa Claus. ☐

34 **Mark the wrong ending.**

Before Christmas families in Great Britain …

a) write a lot of Christmas cards. ☐
b) get a lot of Christmas cards. ☐
c) sell a lot of Christmas cards. ☐
c) decorate their homes with Christmas cards. ☐

Extra tip

35 **Welcher Tipp ist am wenigsten zu empfehlen?**

Ich bereite mich am besten auf eine Klassenarbeit vor, …

a) indem ich möglichst eine Woche vorher einen Plan aufstelle. ☐
b) indem ich den Lernstoff auf mehrere Tage verteile. ☐
c) indem ich das Gelernte ein paar Mal wiederhole. ☐
d) indem ich versuche, alles einen Tag vor der Arbeit zu lernen. ☐

Vocabulary

1 Which one is not made of *cotton*?

a) a shirt ☐
b) fashion ☐
c) a skirt ☐
d) socks ☐

2 Which of these is never *red*?

a) blood ☐
b) rose ☐
c) milk ☐
d) skin ☐

3 Find the right word.

You use a … to find the meaning of a word.
a) dictionary ☐
b) wordbook ☐
c) workbook ☐
d) magazine ☐

4 Which one is correct?

At a restaurant you ask for the …
a) card. ☐
b) ticket. ☐
c) menu. ☐
d) map. ☐

5 Three in one. Which word describes all the other three?

a) platform ☐
b) railway station ☐
c) passengers ☐
d) train ☐

6 **British English (BE) and American English (AE): Which pair isn't correct?**

a) BE: lorry – AE: truck ☐
b) BE: motorway – AE: highway ☐
c) BE: petrol – AE: gas ☐
d) BE: town centre – AE: city ☐

7 **Which ordinal number is not written correctly?**

a) 12th = twelfth ☐
b) 22nd = twenty-second ☐
c) 30th = thirtieth ☐
d) 99th = ninety-nineth ☐

8 ***A married woman's man is her …***

a) man. ☐
b) male. ☐
c) husband. ☐
d) mister. ☐

9 **Wie gefällt dir das neue *Layout*, d.h. … der Zeitung?**

a) der Name ☐
b) die Text- und Bildgestaltung ☐
c) die Farbe ☐
d) der Preis ☐

Language

10 **Mark the word that doesn't have an [ɔ:].**

a) board ☐
b) road ☐
c) talk ☐
d) horse ☐

11 **Which pair of words sounds the same?**

a) mile – male ☐
b) male – mail ☐
c) mail – meal ☐
d) meal – mile ☐

12 **What does *e.g.* not mean?**

a) for example ☐
b) electric guitar ☐
c) for instance ☐
d) exempli gratia ☐

13 **Complete this proverb.**

Make hay while …
a) you are young. ☐
b) the sun shines. ☐
c) the farmer is in the fields. ☐
d) your parents sleep. ☐

14 **Complete this proverb.**

As you make your bed, you …
a) must lie on it. ☐
b) must sleep in it. ☐
c) will dream about it. ☐
d) will sit on it. ☐

Reading

15 **Where can you read this sign?**

RETURN YOUR TRAY HERE

a) in a restaurant ☐
b) in a supermarket ☐
c) in hospital ☐
d) in the school cafeteria ☐

16 **Read the label and then decide what it says.**

a) You can eat this yoghurt only until 26th October. ☐
b) Don't eat this yoghurt before 26th October. ☐
c) This yoghurt was made on 26th October. ☐
d) You mustn't buy this yoghurt until 26th October. ☐

YOGHURT
"CREAMY"
WITH BANANAS
USE BY 26 OCTOBER

17 **Find the information which is not given in this ad.**

a) The handlebars and frame are made of steel. ☐
b) You pay £112 less. ☐
c) The BMX is ten years old. ☐
d) The wheels and brakes are made of aluminium. ☐

18 **Which information is the only correct one?**

a) The pedals are for riders with very big feet only. ☐
b) Kirsty's Bike Shop offers all types of bikes. ☐
c) The seat is extremely hard. ☐
d) The guarantee includes all parts of the bike. ☐

KBS – ALL KINDS OF BIKES

- **This month's special offer: BMX Bike: Type: Back Cat 2010**
- **Steel frame**
- **Steel handlebars type: Hi-Tech "R^2"**
- **Saddle: padded* seat, type "Jump"**
- **Alu-V-brakes**
- **Wheels: aluminum black**
- **304 front and rear tyres**
- **Extras: „Bigfoot" pedals**
- **Price: ~~£311~~ £199**
- **10 years guarantee on frame and handlebars.**
- **Call or e-mail: Kirsty's Bike Shop, Greenwich/London kbs@greenwich.com**

*padded – gepolstert

Communication

19 **Which word is correct?**

It's … that I can't use my computer at the moment.

a) a pitty ☐
b) fair ☐
c) bored ☐
d) excited ☐

20 **Which question is not correct?**

a) How do you say *Abendbrot* in English? ☐
b) How is *Apfelsaft* in English? ☐
d) How do you spell *juice*? ☐
c) What does *cucumber* mean in German? ☐

21 **Which answer is not correct?**

What's the matter? …

a) I've got a bad headache. ☐
b) My back hurts. ☐
c) You should see a doctor. ☐
d) I feel ill. ☐

22 **What's the best way to *finish* a letter?**

a) What a nice idea to send me a postcard from your holiday resort in Italy. ☐
b) Thank you for your recent letter. ☐
c) I am looking forward to hearing from you soon. ☐
d) It was a really good idea to send me a letter. ☐

Grammar

23 **Spot the wrong form.**

a) go - went - gone ☐
b) do- did - done ☐
c) win - won - wone ☐
d) be - was/were - been ☐

24 **Which question word is not correct?**

a) *What's* Bradley's favourite country? - Sweden. ☐
b) *Who* did he visit there? - His uncle and aunt. ☐
c) *When* was he there? - Last August. ☐
d) *Where* did he meet there? - His Swedish friends. ☐

25 **Which comparison is correct?**

The USA is … England.

a) much larger then ☐
b) many larger than ☐
c) much largest than ☐
d) much larger than ☐

26 **Choose the correct question tag.**

You've seen the new film, …

a) haven't you? ☐
b) won't you? ☐
c) don't you? ☐
d) didn't you? ☐

27 **Which verb form is correct?**

Last April Jane's class … on a school trip.

a) have gone ☐
b) went ☐
c) has gone ☐
d) didn't went ☐

28 **Which word is correct?**

Two of Jane's friends lost … mobiles on the trip.

a) there ☐
b) their ☐
c) they're ☐
d) they ☐

29 **Find the sentence with the wrong word.**

a) We went *to* an open air concert last week. ☐
b) It wasn't *two* expensive. ☐
c) Our friends went there, *too*. ☐
d) *Two* of them didn't get tickets. ☐

Culture

30 **What's Queen Elizabeth II's surname?**

a) Buckingham. ☐
b) Great Britain. ☐
c) Mountbatten-Windsor. ☐
d) She hasn't got a surname. ☐

31 ***When Queen Elizabeth II is in London she lives in …***

a) the Houses of Parliament. ☐
b) Buckingham Palace. ☐
c) the Tower of London. ☐
d) Westminster Abbey. ☐

32 **Mark the wrong statement.**

a) Elizabeth II has been Queen since 1952. ☐
b) Elizabeth II and her husband Philip have four children: Anne, Charles, Andrew and Edward. ☐
c) The Queen has got seven grandchildren. ☐
d) Elizabeth II was 65 years old in 2005. ☐

33 **Who was it?**

a) Marilyn Monroe ☐
b) Madonna ☐
c) Hilary Clinton ☐
d) Diana, Princess of Wales ☐

She was born on July 1, 1961 at Sandringham, Norfolk, England. After some years in England she finished school in Switzerland. Then she worked as a nursery school teacher at the Young England School in Pimlico, London.
On July 29, 1981 she married Prince Charles at St Paul's Cathedral, London. 15 years later they got divorced. On August 31st, 1997 she died in a traffic accident in Paris, France. Her two sons, Prince William and Prince Harry organized a huge live concert at the Wembley Stadium in summer 2007 to remember her.

34 **Which statement is wrong?**

a) She went to schools in England and Switzerland. ☐
b) She worked as an English teacher in Pimlico, London. ☐
c) She was married for fifteen years. ☐
d) When she died she was only 37 years old. ☐

Extra Tip

35 **Welches Lernverhalten ist nicht sinnvoll?**

a) Ich arbeite ab und zu mit einem Freund. ☐
b) Ich mache mir im Unterricht Notizen, um zu Hause wiederholen zu können. ☐
c) Wenn ich bei einer Aufgabe unsicher bin, lass ich es lieber bleiben. ☐
d) Wenn ich etwas nicht verstanden habe, frage ich nach. ☐

Vocabulary

1 Which one is not made of *fruit*?

a) jam ☐
b) porridge ☐
c) juice ☐
d) wine ☐

2 From slow to fast. Tick the correct order.

a) by bike → on foot → by plane → by car ☐
b) on foot → by car → by bike → by plane ☐
c) by car → on foot → by bike → by plane ☐
d) on foot → by bike → by car → by plane ☐

3 Three in one. Which word describes all the other three?

a) knee ☐
b) foot ☐
c) leg ☐
d) toe ☐

4 British English (BE) and American English (AE): Which pair isn't correct?

a) BE: shop – AE: store ☐
b) BE: sweets – AE: bonbons ☐
c) BE: chips – AE: French fries ☐
c) BE: tin – AE: can ☐

5 Which is the odd one?

a) first ☐
b) twice ☐
c) three times ☐
d) four times ☐

6 **Which girl's first name is not the name of a flower?**

a) Daisy ☐
b) Nellie ☐
c) Lily ☐
d) Rose ☐

7 ***Ron is married to Jill. Jill's mother is Ron's …***

a) stepmother. ☐
b) mother tongue. ☐
c) mother-of-law. ☐
d) mother in-law. ☐

8 **Kreuze die falsche Bedeutung an.**

Wie gefällt dir das neue *Outfit, d.h.* … unserer Mannschaft?
a) das Trikot ☐
b) die Werbung auf den Trikots ☐
c) der Trainingsanzug ☐
d) die Sportkleidung ☐

9 **Which explanation is correct?**

B.C. means …
a) British cars. ☐
b) Before Christ. ☐
c) Birth Control. ☐
d) British Christmas. ☐

Language

10 **Find the odd one.**

a) tourist ☐
b) dentist ☐
c) florist ☐
d) computer specialist ☐

11 **Which word has no [ɑ:] ?**

a) market ☐
b) garden ☐
c) fun ☐
d) cartoon ☐

12 **Which pair of words sound the same?**

a) far – fare ☐
b) fare – fair ☐
c) fair – fear ☐
d) fear – far ☐

13 **Complete this proverb.**

He who laughs last laughs …

a) loudly. ☐
b) the loudest. ☐
c) with his friends. ☐
d) at his friends. ☐

14 **Complete this proverb.**

Laughter is the best …

a) start to your day. ☐
b) food. ☐
c) medicine. ☐
d) answer to a silly question. ☐

Reading

15 **Where can you read this sign?**

BEWARE OF THE DOG

a) At the doctor's. ☐
b) On a garden gate. ☐
c) In an old castle. ☐
d) At the hairdresser's. ☐

16 **Find the information which is not given in this ad.**

a) The flat has a bathroom. ☐
b) The rent per month is £516. ☐
c) You can wash your clothes in the kitchen. ☐
d) You can park your car in front of the house. ☐

17 **Which information is given in the text?**

a) You can use the small front garden. ☐
b) You can use an electric oven in the kitchen. ☐
c) The flat is rather old-fashioned. ☐
d) It's outside the town. ☐

GREENWICH, NELSON ROAD:

Modern one bedroom flat in the centre of Greenwich.
Nice sitting room, modern kitchen with an electric oven and a breakfast bar; white bathroom with shower and washing machine; gas central heating; small balcony; off street parking; just three minutes to the bus station.
Rent: £129 per week;
Contact: J. Pepper and S. Alt Estate Agents, Greenwich, Ph. 344 768 551

18 **Read this notice and then decide which statement is correct.**

CYCLISTS MUST SLOW DOWN FOR PEDESTRIANS HERE

a) If there are people on this path, cyclists should ride more slowly. ☐
b) If there are people on this path, all cyclists must leave the cycle path. ☐
c) People should leave the path at once if they see a cyclist. ☐
d) People should walk more slowly if there is a cyclist on this path. ☐

Communication

19 ***You want to know the price of something.*** **Which question is correct?**

a) How much costs it? ☐
b) How much is it? ☐
c) How many does it cost? ☐
d) Which price has it got? ☐

20 **What's the correct answer?**

What would you like, John? …
a) I will an ice cream, please. ☐
b) I want an ice cream, please. ☐
c) I want to have an ice cream, please. ☐
d) I'd like an ice cream, please. ☐

21 Which answer doesn't fit?

Could I borrow your keys for a moment? …

a) Yes, of course. ☐
b) I'm sorry, I need them. ☐
c) Yes, here you are. ☐
d) I'm afraid, I can't. ☐

22 Which of these sentences do you use to *start* a letter?

a) Please write back as soon as possible. ☐
b) That's all for today. ☐
c) I was surprised to read that you have left school. ☐
d) I hope to hear from you soon. ☐

Grammar

23 Spot the wrong form.

a) sit - sat - sat ☐
b) say - said - said ☐
c) read - red- read ☐
d) see- saw - seen ☐

24 Which preposition is correct?

We often have guests … Saturdays.

a) at ☐
b) in ☐
c) on ☐
d) to ☐

25 Which relative pronoun is correct?

A shop assistant is a person … sells things in a shop.

a) whose ☐
b) who ☐
c) which ☐
d) where ☐

26 **Which sentence is correct?**

a) After school we often meet us. ☐
b) We meet often after school. ☐
c) After school we meet us often. ☐
d) We often meet after school. ☐

27 **Which short answer is correct?**

Does your sister like hard rock? …
a) Yes, she do. ☐
b) No, she not. ☐
c) No, she does. ☐
d) No, she doesn't. ☐

28 **Which word isn't written correctly?**

a) Kate and Bradley met last year and from *then* on they were friends. ☐
b) Bradley said, "My love for you is bigger *than* the ocean." ☐
c) They travelled to Italy first, *then* they went on to Malta. ☐
d) The trip cost more *then* 500 pounds. ☐

29 **Find the wrong sentence.**

a) We have a cat. *It's* twelve weeks old now. ☐
b) Our cat gets *it's* food twice a day. ☐
c) We all like *its* face. ☐
d) *It's* so sweet. ☐

Culture

30 **Which date is not correct for these days in Britain?**

a) St. Valentine's Day is on 14th February. ☐
b) St. Patrick's Day is on 17th March. ☐
c) Halloween is on 31st October. ☐
d) Guy Fawkes' Day is on 25th December. ☐

31 **Mark the wrong statement.**

St. Patrick …

a) is Ireland's greatest king. ☐
b) is Ireland's greatest saint. ☐
c) was born in 387 AD. ☐
d) built the first churches in Ireland. ☐

32 **Who was this man?**

a) Lord Robert Baden-Powell ☐
b) Prime Minister Winston Churchill ☐
c) Captain James Cook ☐
d) Nobel prize winner Nelson Mandela ☐

He was a lieutenant-general in the British Army, a writer, and he founded the boy scouts*.
After school he was in the British Army from 1876 until 1910 in India and Africa. Some of his military books, which he wrote for military and scout training in his African years, were read by many boys. In 1908 "Scouting for Boys" was published. He tested his ideas in a camping trip on Brownsea Island in 1907, which was the beginning of Scouting. He lived his last years in Nyeri, Kenya, where he died in 1941.

**boy scouts* – Pfadfinder

33 **Read the text again and find the wrong statement.**

a) He served in the British Army for 34 years. ☐
b) Many boys and girls liked to read his books about military training. ☐
c) He was the founder of the boy scouts. ☐
d) Before he wrote his book "Scouting for Boys" he tested his ideas. ☐

34 ***Boy scouts try to do …***

a) a good deed every day. ☐
b) a good deed every year. ☐
c) a good deed every Sunday. ☐
d) ten good deeds every day. ☐

Extra tip

35 **Welcher Tipp macht am wenigsten Sinn?**

Wenn ich die Bedeutung eines Wortes nicht kenne, …

a) versuche ich den Sinn des Satzes auch ohne das Wort zu verstehen. ☐
b) denke ich mir einfach eine Bedeutung aus. ☐
c) versuche ich über ähnliche Wörter an die Bedeutung heranzukommen. ☐
d) schlage ich notfalls die Bedeutung in einem Wörterbuch nach. ☐

Vocabulary

1 Which one is never made of *wood*?

a) cupboard ☐
b) shelf ☐
c) chimney ☐
d) chair ☐

2 Find the odd one.

a) ferry ☐
b) truck ☐
c) lorry ☐
d) van ☐

3 From small to big. Tick the correct order.

a) sentence → word → letter → text ☐
b) text → word → letter → sentence ☐
c) letter → word → sentence → text ☐
d) word → text → letter → sentence ☐

4 Three in one. Which word describes all the other three?

a) plates ☐
b) dishes ☐
c) cups ☐
d) bowls ☐

5 British English (BE) and American English (AE): Which pair isn't correct?

a) BE: holiday – AE: vacation ☐
b) BE: luggage – AE: baggage ☐
c) BE: rucksack – AE: suitcase ☐
d) BE: campsite – AE: campground ☐

6 ***A dozen is …***

a) six. ☐
b) twelve. ☐
c) twenty. ☐
d) one hundred. ☐

7 **Which adjective isn't correct?**

a) the Chinese Wall ☐
b) Switzerland chocolate ☐
c) a Japanese motorbike ☐
d) a Greek statue ☐

8 **Who was a member of your family and lived a long time ago?**

a) grandson ☐
b) grandchild ☐
c) great-grandmother ☐
d) grand piano ☐

9 **Kreuze die richtige Bedeutung an.**

Tausende von Menschen konnten die Fußball-WM 2006 durch *public viewing*, d.h. auf Großbildleinwänden … verfolgen.

a) in Einkaufszentren ☐
b) in Kinos ☐
c) in Gaststätten ☐
c) auf öffentlichen Plätzen ☐

Language

10 **Which word is not pronounced with [ɪə]?**

a) clear ☐
b) dear ☐
c) bear ☐
d) hear ☐

11 **Which pair of words sounds the same?**

a) whole – hall ☐
b) hall – who'll ☐
c) who'll – hole ☐
d) hole – whole ☐

12 **Which explanation is wrong?**

a) USA → United States of America ☐
b) UN → United Nationalities ☐
c) UK → United Kingdom ☐
d) EU → European Union ☐

13 **Complete this proverb.**

All that glitters is not …

a) metal. ☐
b) silver. ☐
c) gold. ☐
d) iron. ☐

14 **Complete this proverb.**

Every cloud has a … lining.

a) metallic ☐
b) silver ☐
c) golden ☐
d) iron ☐

Reading

15 **Where can you read this sign?**

a) In a youth hostel. ☐
b) In a gymnasium. ☐
c) Under a bridge. ☐
d) In a cinema. ☐

16 **What does this notice mean?**

STONEWATERS BOOKSTORES'
SPECIAL OFFER THIS WEEK
BUY TWO BOOKS AND GET ONE FREE

a) If you buy three books, you'll get two free ones. ☐
b) You have to buy two books and then you will get one without paying. ☐
c) You have to pay for three books. ☐
d) Stonewaters makes this special offer once a year. ☐

17 **Read this ad and then tick the wrong sentence.**

a) It's a four-star hostel. ☐
b) 200 people can sleep in the hostel. ☐
c) Up to six people can use the largest rooms. ☐
d) There are four three-bed rooms. ☐

YOUTH HOSTEL INVERNESS **

Youth Hostel Inverness ****
Victoria Drive,
Inverness, IV2 3QB

Ph: 0870 004 1127
Central Bookings: 0870 1 55 32 55

Facilities

Beds per room	Number of rooms
2	2
3	4
4	4
6	24
Total beds	176

18 **Look at the facilities. Which information is wrong?**

a) The next bus station and the railway station are not far away. ☐
b) The hostel is open to handicapped people. ☐
c) The next airport is only eight miles away. ☐
d) The supermarket is in the hostel. ☐

Communication

19 ***You want to know how long you will have to wait.* What can you say?**

a) How long will it need? ☐
b) How long will it take? ☐
c) How long is the duration? ☐
d) How long lasts it? ☐

20 **Which reply is not correct?**

Excuse me, is your name really Sunny Rain? …

a) No, it's Susan Kane. ☐
b) And yours? ☐
c) Pardon? ☐
d) It's Susan Kane. ☐

21 **What's the only possible answer?**

Would you like to see the new Harry Potter film tonight? …

a) Perhaps, why not? ☐
b) Yes, I do. ☐
c) I think you're right. ☐
d) I don't know, but I'm bit tired. ☐

22 **Which sentence is the best to *finish* a letter?**

a) It'll be nice to meet you and your family in August. ☐
b) I am really sorry I did not write earlier. ☐
c) Well, that's all for today. ☐
d) I am sorry that I couldn't answer your letter sooner. ☐

Grammar

23 **Spot the wrong form.**

a) put - put -put ☐
b) cut - cut - cut ☐
c) hit - hit - hit ☐
d) built - built - built ☐

24 **Which plural form is wrong?**

a) He always watches the *news* at 8 p.m. ☐
b) I need some more *information*. ☐
c) Bradley likes *fruit* and vegetables. ☐
d) There were five *sheeps* on the road. ☐

25 **Which conjunction is correct?**

Kate went surfing on her first day in California … she had a cold.

a) or ☐
b) if ☐
c) although ☐
d) because ☐

26 **Which word is correct?**

Bradley: Kate, stop talking, please. –
Kate: I didn't say … , Bradley.

a) nothing ☐
b) anything ☐
c) something ☐
d) everything ☐

27 **Find the correct sentence.**

a) He has worked in Portugal for 15 months. ☐
b) He works in Portugal for 15 months. ☐
c) He has worked in Portugal since 15 months. ☐
d) He worked in Portugal since 15 months. ☐

28 **Which simple present form is wrong?**

a) Every Monday Tom White, the famous basketball player, *flys* to Italy. ☐
b) He *plays* basketball there. ☐
c) His manager *carries* all his luggage. ☐
d) Every morning his manager *lays* the table and then they have breakfast. ☐

29 **Which present progressive form is wrong?**

a) Look, Bradley is *running* after his dog. ☐
b) He is *coming* home from work. ☐
c) Grandpa is *takeing* the dog for a walk. ☐
d) The children are *lying* in the grass. ☐

Culture

30 **Mark the wrong country.**

People don't drive on the left in …

a) the USA. ☐
b) Great Britain. ☐
c) Australia. ☐
d) South Africa. ☐

31 **Mark the wrong statement.**

In countries where people drive on the left …

a) drivers sit on the right side in their car. ☐

b) the tank is always on the right side of the car. ☐

c) the driver has to overtake from the right. ☐

d) pedestrians have to look to the right side first before they cross the road. ☐

32 **Who was it?**

a) Oliver Hardy ☐

b) Stan Laurel ☐

c) Oleg Popov ☐

d) Charlie Chaplin ☐

He was an English comedy actor and musician. Some people say he was the best clown ever. He also wrote the stories for his own films and produced them. He worked in the entertainment business all his life – over 65 years, until his death at the age of eighty-eight in 1977. In his films he usually wore a tight coat, oversized trousers and shoes, a bowler hat and carried a bamboo stick.

33 **Read the text again and find the wrong statement.**

a) He was a great English entertainer. ☐

b) In his free time he often wore a tight coat, big shoes and a bowler hat. ☐

c) He also was a famous film producer. ☐

d) He acted as a clown. ☐

34 **What's wrong?**

His early films were …

a) black-and-white films. ☐

b) silent films. ☐

c) short films. ☐

d) the first films on colour TV. ☐

Extra tip

35 **Welcher Tipp is deiner Meinung nach am wenigsten sinnvoll?**

Wenn ich etwas Englisches anhöre und Aufgaben dazu lösen möchte, …

a) versuche ich zunächst herauszufinden, um was es geht (wer?, was?, wo?, wann?) ☐

b) lese ich die Aufgaben vorher und achte dann speziell auf diese Inhalte. ☐

c) achte ich darauf, jedes einzelne Wort zu verstehen. ☐

d) nutze ich auch Hintergrundgeräusche auf der CD, um die Situation besser zu verstehen. ☐

Vocabulary

1 Which of these is never *soft*?

a) water ☐
b) cream ☐
c) stone ☐
d) baby's skin ☐

2 Spot the false place of work.

a) captain ⟷ ship ☐
b) doctor ⟷ shop ☐
c) headmaster ⟷ school ☐
d) manager ⟷ company ☐

3 What do people usually do there?

a) bank – change money ☐
b) church – study ☐
c) factory – build machines ☐
d) library – lend books ☐

4 Three in one. Which word describes all the other three?

a) sausages ☐
b) food ☐
c) rice ☐
d) bread ☐

5 British English (BE) and American English (AE): Which pair isn't correct?

a) BE: parcel – AE: package ☐
b) BE: phone box – AE: pay phone ☐
c) BE: post code – AE: zip code ☐
d) BE: to post a letter – AE: to deliver a letter ☐

6 What's wrong?

a) 8:15 It's quarter past eight. ☐
b) 8:30 It's half nine. ☐
c) 8:35 It's twenty-five to nine. ☐
d) 8:47 It's thirteen minutes to nine. ☐

7 Which currency is not correct?

a) France → euro (€) ☐
b) Great Britain → pound (£) ☐
c) USA → dollar ($) ☐
d) Japan → lira (L) ☐

8 Find the wrong one.

Young children call their …
a) father *daddy*. ☐
b) mother *mummy*. ☐
c) grandmother *grandy*. ☐
d) aunt *auntie*. ☐

9 Beim Basketball entscheiden jedes Jahr die *Play-offs*, d.h. … die Meisterschaft.

a) die Spiele in der Aufstiegsrunde ☐
b) die Spiele in der Vorrunde ☐
c) die Freiwürfe ☐
d) die Entscheidungsspiele der besten Mannschaften ☐

Language

10 Which word doesn't have an [aʊ]?

a) show ☐
b) crowd ☐
c) blouse ☐
d) round ☐

11 Which pair of words sounds the same?

a) word – world ☐
b) world – wood ☐
c) wood – would ☐
d) would – word ☐

12 Which long form is wrong?

a) Mrs Miller = Misses Miller ☐
b) Mr Smith = Manager Smith ☐
c) Ms Italy = Miss Italy ☐
d) MS = Mississippi ☐

13 Complete this proverb.

Don't put all your … in one basket.

a) coins ☐
b) eggs ☐
c) pencils ☐
d) sweets ☐

14 Complete this proverb.

Easy come, …

a) easy go. ☐
b) easy gone. ☐
c) hard to get back. ☐
c) hard to leave. ☐

Reading

15 Where can a sign like this not be found?

a) In front of a school. ☐
b) Next to a kindergarten. ☐
c) In a church. ☐
d) 500 metres in front of a youth hostel. ☐

16 **What does this notice mean?**

a) After 11 p.m. the guest has to lock the door. ☐
b) After midnight, please knock at the door. ☐
c) There is no receptionist during the day. ☐
d) The hotel is locked during the night. ☐

THE SUNRISE HOTEL
ENTRANCE LOCKED AT 11 P.M.
PLEASE RING FOR THE RECEPTIONIST
TO OPEN

17 **Read this ad. Which statement is correct?**

a) The Yorkshire Post is England's youngest newspaper. ☐
b) The newspaper's offices are in Leeds. ☐
c) The paper is for readers who are older than 15! ☐
d) The Yorkshire Post is looking for young reporters. ☐

18 **Which information is given in this ad?**

a) You can contact Mrs Morrison by sending an e-mail. ☐
b) You should be 15 or younger to apply for the job. ☐
c) You'll get £ 95 if you do the job for one month. ☐
d) To deliver the paper you must live in York. ☐

The YORKSHIRE POST is one of Britain's oldest newspapers, founded in 1754.
DO YOU WANT MORE POCKET MONEY FOR YOUR NEXT HOLIDAYS?
We are looking for boys and girls (not younger than 15) to do paper rounds in York in the mornings in July and August.
£95 per month
Talk to Carmela Morrison
Wellington Street,
Leeds LS1 1RF Main Office
Tel: 0113 243 2701 or send a fax:
0113 244 3430

Communication

19 ***Can you give me a ring?*** **means . . .**

a) Will you marry me? ☐
b) Could you call me on my phone? ☐
c) Could you give me a present for my birthday? ☐
d) I like jewellery. ☐

20 **Shopping. Which *second* sentence is not correct?**

I'm looking for a sweater. ...
a) Have you got anything in black? ☐
b) Can I try one on? ☐
c) Where's the changing room? ☐
d) Can I look me round? ☐

21 Which reaction is wrong?

Is it OK if I sit here? …

a) Yeah. ☐
b) Yes, sure. ☐
c) Yes, you are. ☐
d) Yes, of course. ☐

22 What's the best way to *start* a letter?

a) It's great to hear about your job in France. ☐
b) Please write as soon as you have time. ☐
c) I'd love to hear more about you. ☐
d) I have to go to the dentist now. ☐

Grammar

23 Spot the wrong form.

a) sleep – slept – slept ☐
b) feel – felt – felt ☐
c) keep – kept – kept ☐
d) leeve – left – left ☐

24 Which preposition isn't used correctly?

a) The new quiz show is on *between* 7 and 8 p.m. ☐
b) The news is *in* TV at 9 p.m. ☐
c) We often watch TV *until* midnight. ☐
d) We never get up *before* 9 a.m. ☐

25 Which one is correct?

May I borrow your MP3 player? I've lost …

a) my. ☐
b) mine. ☐
c) the own. ☐
d) the own one. ☐

26 **Which form of the adverb is wrong?**

a) If I have to write a text *quickly* on my notebook I make a lot of mistakes. ☐
b) Don't worry, computers can *easily* check the spelling. ☐
c) That's true. Perhaps I should write *more carefully*. ☐
d) I know it is not easy, but you must try *hardly*. ☐

27 **Mark the correct tense.**

At the moment seven classes of Thomas Tallis School … a school fete for next month.

a) plan ☐
b) are planning ☐
c) were planning ☐
d) have planned ☐

28 **Two consonants or one? Find the wrong one.**

a) stop – stopped ☐
b) repair – repaired ☐
c) beg – begged ☐
d) plan – planed ☐

29 **Two consonants or one? Find the wrong one.**

a) swim – swimming ☐
b) rain – raining ☐
c) run – runing ☐
d) travel – travelling ☐

Culture

30 **Mark the wrong statement.**

a) The Flag of Scotland is the St. Andrew's Cross. ☐
b) Edinburgh is the capital of Scotland. ☐
c) In Scotland a *lake* is called *loch*. ☐
d) Loch Ness is a famous mountain in Scotland. ☐

31 ***A bagpipe is a traditional Scottish …***

a) big suitcase. ☐
b) musical instrument. ☐
c) pipeline from the North Sea to Aberdeen. ☐
d) song. ☐

32 **Read the text. What was his greatest invention?**

a) electric bulb ☐
b) electric bell ☐
c) torch ☐
d) telephone ☐

Alexander Graham Bell was born in Edinburgh, Scotland, on 3rd March 1847.
He grew up in Edinburgh. As a boy his main interest was the sciences. At the age of 23, he and his parents emigrated to Canada. There Bell studied the human voice and ear. He looked for a method of communication with electricity. Later he became a professor at Boston University, USA. Since his mother and wife were deaf*, he studied deafness to understand their problems better. His studies on hearing and speaking soon led him to his greatest invention. For that he was awarded the first U.S. patent in 1876. Bell died in Canada in 1922.

**deaf* – taub

33 **Read the text again and find the right statement.**

a) Bell was born in Scotland and died in the USA. ☐
b) Both his mother and brother were deaf. ☐
c) Bell always looked for a way to make communication possible by electricity. ☐
d) Without Bell's invention modern communication would be possible. ☐

34 **Guess the wrong fact.**

a) In 1844 Samuel Morse sent the first telephone message. ☐
b) In 1936 the first TV broadcast was made in London. ☐
c) In 1957 a satellite sent information back to earth for the first time. ☐
d) In 1999 the Pentium III processor was introduced. ☐

Extra tip

35 **Welcher Tipp ist deiner Meinung nach unangebracht?**

Ein englisches Gespräch/einen Dialog sollte man …
a) mehrmals von der CD anhören. ☐
b) versuchen nachzusprechen. ☐
c) versuchen im Tonfall nachzuahmen. ☐
d) mehrmals abschreiben. ☐

Vocabulary

1 Which of these is never *striped*?

a) wallpaper ☐
b) newspaper ☐
c) tie ☐
d) zebra ☐

2 Spot the false place of work.

a) a lawyer ⟷ court ☐
b) a waiter ⟷ restaurant ☐
c) a nurse ⟷ hospital ☐
d) a cook ⟷ post office ☐

3 Find the odd one.

Firemen need …
a) a fire engine ☐
b) water ☐
c) a helmet ☐
d) paper ☐

4 You need it to carry your clothes when you travel.

a) a briefcase ☐
b) a purse ☐
c) a suitcase ☐
d) a handbag ☐

5 Three in one. Which word includes all the other three?

a) radio ☐
b) media ☐
c) newspaper ☐
d) TV ☐

6 **British English (BE) and American English (AE): Which pair isn't correct?**

a) BE: engaged – AE: busy ☐
b) BE: mobile (phone) – AE: cell phone ☐
c) BE: to phone someone – AE: to connect someone ☐
d) BE: dialling code – AE: area code ☐

7 **Mark the wrong long form.**

a) 7.95 mm – seven point ninety-five millimetres ☐
b) 15.45 cm – fifteen point forty-five centimetres ☐
c) 0.75 m– oh point seventy-five metres ☐
d) 2.50 ml – two point fifty miles ☐

8 **What's the correct pair?**

husband and …
a) wife ☐
b) woman ☐
c) female ☐
d) lady ☐

9 **Kreuze die falsche Bedeutung an.**

Auf dem *Cover*, d. h. auf … des neuen Buches ist eine herrliche Abbildung der Rocky Mountains.
a) dem Umschlag ☐
b) der Verpackung ☐
c) dem Einband ☐
d) dem Deckel ☐

Language

10 **Which word has no [æ]?**

a) traffic ☐
b) machine ☐
c) racket ☐
d) van ☐

11 **Which pair of words sounds the same?**

a) peas – pays ☐
b) pays – peace ☐
c) peace– piece ☐
d) piece – peas ☐

12 **Which of these is not a school subject?**

a) Physical Education (P.E.) ☐
b) Religious Education (R.E.) ☐
c) Science Fiction (SciFi) ☐
d) Biology (B) ☐

13 **Complete this proverb.**

There's no … like home.

a) location ☐
b) place ☐
c) site ☐
d) spot ☐

14 **Complete this proverb.**

My home is my …

a) palace. ☐
b) villa. ☐
c) residence. ☐
d) castle. ☐

Reading

15 **Where can you read this sign?**

NO SWIMMING WHEN RED FLAG IS FLYING

a) near a swimming pool ☐
b) on the beach ☐
c) in a bathroom ☐
d) on a sailing boat ☐

16 **What does this notice mean?**

IN CASE OF FIRE
USE STAIRS

a) If you use the stairs, you could start a fire. ☐
b) Don't use the stairs, because there is a fire at the moment. ☐
c) If there is a fire in the building, use the stairs. ☐
d) Stairs are dangerous. ☐

17 **Read this ad and then tick the wrong statement.**

The price of £ 259 includes …
a) the flight from England to Austria. ☐
b) accommodation and breakfast for seven days. ☐
c) transfers and guide. ☐
d) a classical concert in Salzburg. ☐

18 **Find the information which is not given in this ad.**

a) You can get a brochure. ☐
b) The head office of the Austrian airline is in Salzburg. ☐
c) You will stay in Austria for one week. ☐
d) There is no extra cost for the tour to Salzburg. ☐

AUSTRIA, 7 DAYS FROM ONLY £ 259
Including:
- **Fly from Stansted, Manchester, or Bristol**
- **Departing: Sundays from July to September 2008**
- **Transfers/English and German speaking guide**
- **7 nights' accommodation in a nice hotel near Mayerhofen**
- **Continental breakfast and …**

A FREE TOUR TO MAGICAL SALZBURG
Only available if booked by 31st May 2008.
Book now and call for brochure
0871-871-0071
www.austriangetaways.co.uk

Communication

19 **Which one is correct?**

Don't forget to take your anorak with you. It looks … rain.
a) how ☐
b) out like ☐
c) like ☐
d) as ☐

20 ***You didn't understand your English partner.* What can you say?**

a) Would you please talk a bit slowlier? ☐
b) Don't speak so quick. ☐
c) Could you speak more slowly, please? ☐
d) Can you say it slower? ☐

21 **Which reaction does not suit?**

Would you like to go swimming with me tomorrow? …

a) I'd love to, but I'm afraid I can't. ☐
b) Yes, please. ☐
c) Good idea, but what about next week? ☐
d) Sorry, but I don't really want to do anything tomorrow. ☐

22 **Which of these sentences do you use to *finish* an e-mail?**

a) Hoping to hear from you soon. ☐
b) I thought I should reply at once. ☐
c) In your e-mail you told me about your holiday plans. ☐
d) Sorry I didn't answer sooner but I was in hospital for one week. ☐

Grammar

23 **Spot the wrong form.**

a) chose – chose – chosen ☐
b) speak – spoke – spoken ☐
c) steal – stole – stolen ☐
d) wake – woke – woken ☐

24 **Prepositions. Which sentence is correct?**

a) Kate is very good *in* Spanish. ☐
b) She studied Spanish *at* university in Barcelona. ☐
c) She is sure Madrid is the most beautiful place *on* the world. ☐
d) She always looks very happy *on* all photos that Bradley took. ☐

25 **Which reflexive pronoun is correct?**

Kate had a nice time in Bath. She enjoyed … very much there.

a) itself ☐
b) herself ☐
c) themselves ☐
d) yourself ☐

26 **Spot the wrong negation.**

a) Kate says, "I like coffee but I *don't* like tea." ☐
b) Bradley says, "There's a party next week but we *aren't going*." ☐
c) Kate watched TV yesterday, but she *didn't see* the news. ☐
d) Bradley is very tired. He *don't want* to go out this evening. ☐

27 **Which verb is correct?**

Last week the pupils at Thomas Tallis School … their school hall.
a) have decorated ☐
b) decorated ☐
c) decorate ☐
d) are going to decorate ☐

28 **Find the wrong one. One *l* or *double l*?**

a) always ☐
b) all right ☐
c) although ☐
d) alltogether ☐

29 **Find the wrong one. One *l* or *double l*?**

a) till ☐
b) untill ☐
c) full ☐
d) wonderful ☐

Culture

30 **Mark the wrong statement.**

a) The capital of Wales is Belfast. ☐
b) The words *"Croeso I Gymru"* mean *"Welcome to Wales."* ☐
c) The national flag of Wales is The Red Dragon. ☐
d) The longest town name in the world can be found in Wales: It is ☐

LLANFAIRPWLLGWYNGYLLGOGERYCHWYRNDROBWLLLLANTYSILIOGOGOGOCH

ST MARYS CHURCH IN THE HOLLOW OF THE WHITE HAZEL NEAR TO THE RAPID WHIRLPOOL OF LLANTYSILIO OF THE RED CAVE

31 **Which information about Wales is not true?**

a) The head of state in Wales is Queen Elizabeth II. ☐
b) Charles, the Prince of Wales, was born in Wales. ☐
c) 21% of the people in Wales say they can speak Welsh. ☐
d) The highest mountain in Wales is called Snowdon (1085 m). ☐

32 **Who was it?**

There are many stories about him and his knights, but no real facts. If he ever existed, it was probably after the Romans left Britain. That was in the 5th or 6th century.
The beginning of this legend was in Wales. He was probably the leader of the Britons. They say that he never lost a battle against the Saxons. The stories about his knights of the Round Table have lived on to the present day.

a) William the Conqueror ☐
b) Prince William ☐
c) King Arthur ☐
d) Henry VIII ☐

33 **Read the text again and find the wrong statement.**

a) The Saxons could not defeat him. ☐
b) Not all stories about him are real facts. ☐
c) Many people still sit at the Round Table today. ☐
d) Historians think he lived in the 5th or 6th century. ☐

34 **Background knowledge about knights. Guess what's wrong.**

a) Training to become a knight started at the age of seven. ☐
b) At the age of 15 or 16 the boys learned how to fight on horseback. ☐
c) Knights fought for the peasants* and they gave them food and drinks. ☐
d) Knights protected the peasants*. ☐

**peasants* – Kleinbauern

Extra tip

35 **Welche Aussage ist falsch?**

In einem Wörterbuch finde ich …
a) die Leitwörter jeweils am oberen Rand. ☐
b) Wörter mit mehreren Bedeutungen in alphabetischer Reihenfolge. ☐
c) die internationale Lautschrift zur Aussprache jedes englischen Wortes. ☐
d) ausführliche Texte zur englischen und amerikanischen Landeskunde. ☐

Vocabulary

1 Which of these is never *spotted*?

a) dog ☐
b) cow ☐
c) dictionary ☐
d) dress ☐

2 Which place of work is wrong?

a) actor ⟷ theatre ☐
b) travel agent ⟷ plane ☐
c) receptionist ⟷ hotel ☐
d) designer ⟷ studio ☐

3 Mark the correct verb.

Before a plane takes off you must … your seat belt.

a) close ☐
b) shut ☐
c) pull ☐
d) fasten ☐

4 *You need a … to clean your teeth.*

a) paintbrush ☐
b) toothbrush ☐
c) comb ☐
d) pencil ☐

5 Three in one. Which word describes all the other three?

a) actor ☐
b) stage ☐
c) theatre ☐
d) seat ☐

6 British English (BE) and American English (AE): Which pair isn't correct?

a) BE: trousers – AE: jeans ☐
b) BE: football – AE: soccer ☐
c) BE: match – AE: game ☐
d) BE: athletics – AE: track and field ☐

7 Find the wrong definition.

a) 10 years is a decade. ☐
b) 50 years is a semi-century. ☐
c) 100 years is a century. ☐
d) 1,000 years is a millennium. ☐

8 *Two babies born at the same time to the same mother are called …*

a) a double. ☐
b) a duo. ☐
c) twins. ☐
d) bi-babies. ☐

9 Kreuze die falsche Bedeutung an.

Durch *Recycling* können wertvolle Rohstoffe … werden.
a) wieder verwertet ☐
b) abgebaut ☐
c) eingespart ☐
c) in den Produktionskreislauf zurückgeführt ☐

Language

10 Which word has no [i:z]?

a) knees ☐
b) police ☐
c) cheese ☐
d) keys ☐

11 **In which word is the letter *h* not spoken?**

a) horse ☐
b) hospital ☐
c) honest ☐
d) heart ☐

12 **Which of these explanations is wrong?**

a) 10 yd = 10 yards ☐
b) 60° F = 60 degrees Fahrenheit ☐
c) 30 in = 30 inches ☐
d) 40 P = 40 pounds ☐

13 **Complete this proverb.**

Practice makes …

a) the master. ☐
b) you better. ☐
c) perfect. ☐
d) you successful. ☐

14 **Complete this proverb.**

Fine feathers make fine …

a) birds. ☐
b) feet. ☐
c) people. ☐
d) hair. ☐

Reading

15 **Where can't you read these signs?**

a) at the entrance of a football stadium ☐
b) at the railway station ☐
c) at the airport ☐
d) at the bus stop ☐

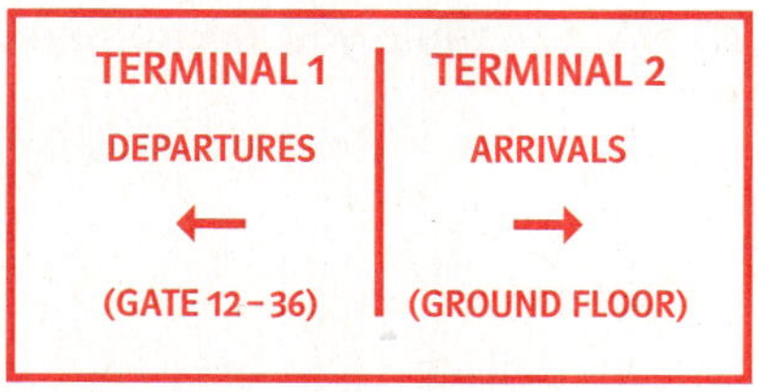

16 **What does this notice mean?**

a) The lifts in the department store are out of order today. ☐
b) A film team is making a film at the moment. ☐
c) People who take things without paying will be taken to court. ☐
d) People who steal things are directly sent to prison. ☐

CAMERAS
IN ALL OUR DEPARTMENTS
SHOPLIFTERS WILL BE PROSECUTED

17 **Which information is not correct?**

a) You can order shoes or boots for less than £40. ☐
b) The pyjamas for girls are reduced £7.50. ☐
c) Order the twin pack of pyjamas and you save 20%. ☐
d) You can only buy the socks in pairs of two. ☐

18 **Tick the correct statement.**

The army parka is … the washed parka for girls.

a) bigger than ☐
b) less expensive than ☐
c) more expensive than ☐
d) as expensive as ☐

ROBBINS AND BENSON, LONDON

SUMMER SALE 10 TO 25 PER CENT LESS

Girls
- **Dresses:**
  T-shirt dress ~~£32~~ £26
- **Outerwear:**
  Fleece anorak ~~£32~~ £26
  Washed parka ~~£39~~ £25
- **Trousers:**
  Embellished jeans ~~£36~~ £22
  Fun cargos ~~£32~~ £19
- **Nightwear:**
  Pyjamas "Dream" ~~£30~~ £22.50
- **Shoes and boots:**
  Now from £26 to £39.95 only

Boys
- **Accessories:**
  Socks (three pairs) ~~£12~~ £8
- **Outerwear:**
  Fleece anorak ~~£32~~ £26
  Army parka ~~£35~~ £21
- **Trousers:**
  Skate jeans ~~£27~~ £19
  Washed down cargos ~~£29~~ £21
- **Nightwear:**
  Twin pack pyjamas ~~£26~~ £20.80
- **Shoes and boots:**
  Now from £26 to £39.95 only

Communication

19 **Which question is correct?**

a) What's the hour? ☐
b) What time is it? ☐
c) What's the clock? ☐
d) Can you give me the time? ☐

20 **At the table you ask someone for the sugar.**

Can you … me the sugar, please?

a) fetch ☐
b) bring ☐
c) deliver ☐
d) pass ☐

21 **Which reaction does not suit?**

I think dancing is great fun. …

a) You have quite right. ☐
b) Yeah, that's right. ☐
c) So do I. ☐
d) Me, too. ☐

22 **Starting and finishing a letter. Which "pair" is not correct?**

a) Dear Mr Brown ⟷ Yours sincerely ☐
b) Dearest Bradley ⟷ With love from … ☐
c) Dear Sir or Madam ⟷ Best wishes ☐
d) Dear Sirs ⟷ Yours faithfully ☐

Grammar

23 **Spot the wrong form.**

a) sing – sang – sung ☐
b) swim – swam – swum ☐
c) beginn – began– begun ☐
d) drink – drank – drunk ☐

24 **Which preposition is not correct?**

a) What time do you usually get *to* school? ☐
b) Do you usually go *by* bus? ☐
c) When did you arrive *in* London yesterday? ☐
d) What time did you arrive *on* the party? ☐

25 **Put in the correct verb.**

Kate, you … You can stay overnight if you want.

a) needn't go. ☐
b) must go. ☐
c) have to go. ☐
d) need to go. ☐

26 **Which verb form is wrong?**

a) If I *don't feel* well tomorrow, I *stay* at home. ☐
b) If you *don't hurry*, you'*ll miss* the bus. ☐
c) What *will* we *do* if it *rains* tomorrow? ☐
d) If you *see* Kate this evening, you'*ll have to ask* her. ☐

27 ***The pupils at Thomas Tallis School … already … their new school play three times.***

a) are … practising ☐
b) were … practising ☐
c) have … practised ☐
d) will … practice ☐

28 **Comparison of adjectives. Find the wrong one.**

a) hot – hotter ☐
b) lucky – luckier ☐
c) big – bigger ☐
d) stupid – stupider ☐

29 ***of*** **or** ***off*****? Find the wrong one.**

a) Bradley eats one bar *of* chocolate every day. ☐
b) You look ill. Why don't you take tomorrow *off*? ☐
c) Sorry, sir, we're out *of* fish today. ☐
d) Take *of* your shoes, please. ☐

Culture

30 **Which of these sights is not in New York?**

a) The Empire State Building ☐
b) Statue of Liberty ☐
c) The White House ☐
d) Times Square ☐

31 **Mark the wrong statement.**

a) New York is also called the Big Apple. ☐
b) Chinatown is a part of New York. ☐
c) More than 8.000.000 people live in New York. ☐
d) The famous World Trade Center was destroyed in 2000. ☐

32 **Who was it?**

a) Roy Lichtenstein ☐
b) Keith Haring ☐
c) Andy Warhol ☐
d) Joseph Beuys ☐

He was a very prominent American pop artist whose work looks like comics. Born on 27th October 1923 in New York City, he attended public school until he was 12. Then he went to the Franklin School in Manhattan for his secondary education. At that time he became more and more interested in art and design. In 1940 he left New York and studied art. After the Second World War he became an art teacher. In the 1950s and 1960s he had a lot of exhibitions at art galleries in New York. During the 1970s and 1980s his work became really famous. He created about 4,500 works of art which look like photographic reproductions. In 1997 he died in New York.

33 **Read the text and find the wrong statement.**

a) When he went to school in New York he was very interested in arts. ☐
b) After World War II he became an art teacher. ☐
c) At the beginning of his career art galleries in New York showed his paintings. ☐
d) He also took more than 4,500 photos. ☐

34 **What does an artist not need?**

a) a brush ☐
b) colours ☐
c) a palette ☐
d) a broom ☐

Extra tip

35 **Welcher Tipp ist am wenigsten sinnvoll?**

Um Vokabeln zu lernen, …
a) genügt die alphabetische Wörterliste im Lehrbuch. ☐
b) sollte man ein Vokabelheft mit einem 3-Spalten-System führen. ☐
c) ist ein Karteikasten mit Karteikarten sehr nützlich. ☐
d) sollte man entsprechende Software zum Lehrwerk nutzen. ☐

Test 9

Vocabulary

1 Which of these is never made of *wool*?

a) kilt ☐
b) blanket ☐
c) tent ☐
d) shirt ☐

2 Spot the wrong word.

I think … has something to do with …

a) a tailor ⟷ clothes ☐
b) a vet ⟷ vegetables ☐
c) a newsagent ⟷ newspapers ☐
d) a dentist ⟷ teeth ☐

3 Mark the odd one.

In a band there is a …

a) rowdy ☐
b) lead singer ☐
c) drummer ☐
d) guitarist ☐

4 Which one is the smallest?

a) a city ☐
b) a village ☐
c) a town ☐
d) a metropolis ☐

5 Three in one. Which word describes all the other three?

a) headache ☐
b) cough ☐
c) illness ☐
d) cold ☐

6 **British English (BE) and American English (AE): Which pair isn't correct?**

a) BE: motorway – AE: motorroad ☐
b) BE: rubbish – AE: garbage ☐
c) BE: underground – AE: subway ☐
d) BE: pavement – AE: sidewalk ☐

7 **How long is a fortnight?**

a) Four nights. ☐
b) Forty nights. ☐
c) Four days. ☐
d) Fourteen days. ☐

8 **Find the correct order.**

a) baby – teenager – child – adult ☐
b) baby – child – teenager – adult ☐
c) child – baby – teenager – adult ☐
d) baby – child – adult – teenager ☐

9 **Der bekannte Fernsehmoderator hat seit Jahren ein positives *Image*.**

Das heißt, … ist gut.
a) sein Ansehen in der Öffentlichkeit ☐
b) sein Einkommen ☐
c) sein Aussehen ☐
d) seine Kondition ☐

Language

10 **Which word is not pronounced with [dʒ]?**

a) cheap ☐
b) jeans ☐
c) Germany ☐
d) jam ☐

11 **Which word is not pronounced with [tʃ]?**

a) chance ☐
b) catch ☐
c) legend ☐
d) future ☐

12 **Which of these abbreviations is not a *weight*?**

a) pt – pint ☐
b) lb – pound ☐
c) oz – ounce ☐
d) kg – kilogram ☐

13 **Complete this proverb.**

Let sleeping dogs …
a) sleep. ☐
b) dream. ☐
c) stretch out. ☐
d) lie. ☐

14 **Complete this proverb.**

Barking dogs seldom …
a) attack you. ☐
b) bite. ☐
c) jump up at you. ☐
d) eat their bones. ☐

Reading

15 **Where can you not read this sign?**

PLEASE, DON'T DISTURB!

a) on a church door ☐
b) on a door of a hotel room ☐
c) at a cash desk in a supermarket ☐
d) on a classroom door ☐

16 **What does this notice mean?**

FEEDING CROCODILES
IS STRICTLY PROHIBITED.
People who throw food at the crocodiles will be asked to take it out of the pool again.

a) Visitors must pick all the food out of the pool. ☐
b) Crocodiles at this zoo are not dangerous. ☐
c) Visitors can go into the pool with the crocodiles. ☐
d) Visitors mustn't feed the crocodiles. ☐

Communication

17 **Read this ad. Then tick the wrong statement.**

a) You have to pay £30 a year for one animal. ☐
b) The soft toy of the adopted animal is for children under eight only. ☐
c) You'll get a photo of your animal. ☐
d) You'll get a newsletter three times a year. ☐

ANIMALS IN DANGER SOCIETY, LONDON

You can adopt an animal in danger for one year. Help give these animals a future for as little as £2.50 a month.
We'll send you our animal adoption pack.
It includes:

- **A soft toy of your animal.**
- **A booklet about your adopted animal.**
- **A photo (with name) of your adopted animal.**
- **A 4-monthly newsletter**

Contact us:
Animals in Danger Society
London NW1 4RY England

18 **Which information is given in this ad?**

a) An adoption of an animal is a nice birthday present for children and adults. ☐
b) All animals have numbers. ☐
c) You will get one free ticket to London Zoo. ☐
d) You can read all about your adopted animal in a short book. ☐

19 ***Can you give me a hand, please?* means ...**

a) Can you help me? ☐
b) Let's shake hands. ☐
c) Can you hold my hand? ☐
d) Let's say goodbye. ☐

20 **You are in town. Which *second* sentence is not correct?**

Excuse me. I'm looking for the nearest underground station. ...
a) How do I get there? ☐
b) Could you say me the way, please? ☐
c) How far is it? ☐
d) Could you show me the way on the map, please? ☐

21 **Which reaction does not fit?**

I think free climbing is rather dangerous. …

a) Do you? I don't. ☐
b) Really? I think it's exciting. ☐
c) I not. ☐
d) I wouldn't say that. ☐

22 **Sending best wishes or greetings. What's not correct?**

a) All our love, Jane and Jason ☐
b) Love from Louisa ☐
c) Best wishes, Diana ☐
d) Greet all, Henry ☐

Grammar

23 **Spot the wrong form.**

a) teech – taught – taught ☐
b) think – thought – thought ☐
c) fight – fought – fought ☐
d) bring – brought – brought ☐

24 **Which sentence needs the preposition *with*?**

a) Rita married … the age of eighteen. ☐
b) What will they buy … all their money? ☐
c) Ron and Rita travelled to Las Vegas … plane. ☐
d) This story is … a young man in Ireland. ☐

25 **Three sentences need *should*. Which sentence needs *shouldn't*?**

a) If you are in London, you … visit Mme. Tussaud's. It's great! ☐
b) If it is too far to walk, you … take the Underground. ☐
c) Do you think I … buy the tickets in advance? ☐
d) Good idea. I think you … wait too long. ☐

26 **Three sentences need *much*. Which sentence needs *many*?**

a) Have you got … luggage? ☐
b) Laura, we haven't seen each other for so … years. ☐
c) Sorry, but I haven't got … time. ☐
d) How … are these biscuits? – They're £1.75. ☐

27 **Find the correct verb for the sentence.**

After the pupils at Thomas Tallis School … more than £500 they sent the money to a charity organization in London.

a) collect ☐
b) are collecting ☐
c) have collected ☐
d) had collected ☐

28 **Capital letters or not? Find the wrong one.**

a) France is west of Germany. ☐
b) the Eastern States of the USA ☐
c) the North Pole ☐
d) South America ☐

29 **Capital letters or not? Find the wrong one.**

a) Once upon a time an old king lived in a castle in Scotland. ☐
b) the king of Spain ☐
c) queen Elizabeth ☐
d) the president of the United States ☐

Culture

30 **Which state does not belong to the USA?**

a) Florida ☐
b) Canada ☐
c) New Mexico ☐
d) California ☐

31 **Mark the wrong statement.**

a) Florida's capital is Miami. ☐
b) Space Shuttles are launched from Cape Canaveral in Florida. ☐
c) Disney World is the greatest tourist attraction in Orlando, Florida. ☐
d) Florida's nickname is Sunshine State. ☐

32 **Who was it?**

a) Iwao Takamoto ☐
b) Charles M. Schulz ☐
c) Walt Disney ☐
d) Matt Groening ☐

He was a famous American film producer and is still well-known for giving his name to many theme parks in the United States, France, Japan and China. He lived from 1901 to 1966. At the age of 26, he had a great idea. When travelling on a train he suddenly remembered the cute little mouse he had as a pet when he was a little boy. He decided to draw the little mouse as a funny cartoon and called it Mortimer. His wife, however, didn't like the long name and called it Mickey. A world star was born.

33 **Read the text again and find the *wrong* statement.**

a) As a boy he often drew his cute little mouse. ☐
b) As a boy he had a cute little mouse. ☐
c) Mortimer was a friendly mouse with big ears. ☐
d) His wife changed the mouse's name to Mickey. ☐

34 **Which of these films did he not produce?**

a) Alice in Wonderland (1951) ☐
b) Living Desert (Die Wüste lebt, 1953) ☐
c) Jaws (Der weiße Hai, 1974) ☐
d) Jungle Book (1967) ☐

Extra tip

35 **Welcher Tipp ist deiner Meinung nach unangebracht?**

Besonders schwierige Vokabeln lerne oder wiederhole ich am besten durch …

a) Merken der Seitenzahl, auf der die Vokabel vorkommt. ☐
b) mehrfaches Abschreiben. ☐
c) lautes Lesen. ☐
d) zusätzliche Eselsbrücken wie z. B. picture words. ☐

Vocabulary

1 Which of these is never *rough*?

a) weather ☐
b) hands ☐
c) voice ☐
d) snow ☐

2 Spot the false word. *A … has something to do with …*

a) butcher ⟷ meat and sausages ☐
b) chemist ⟷ medicine ☐
c) greengrocer ⟷ grass ☐
d) postman ⟷ the mail ☐

3 Mark the wrong one.

Which can't you catch?

a) a ball ☐
b) a train ☐
c) a cold ☐
d) a heat ☐

4 From slow to fast. Tick the correct order.

a) garden snail → cat → human → horse → peregrine falcon → lion → antelope ☐
b) garden snail → human → cat → horse → lion → antelope → peregrine falcon ☐
c) garden snail → horse → human → lion → cat → antelope → peregrine falcon ☐
d) cat → garden snail → horse → human → lion → antelope → peregrine falcon ☐

5 Three in one. Which one produces all the other three?

a) dairy ☐
b) milk ☐
c) cheese ☐
d) butter ☐

6 British English (BE) and American English (AE): Which pair isn't correct?

a) BE: purse – AE: moneybag ☐
b) BE: farm – AE: ranch ☐
c) BE: surname– AE: last name ☐
d) BE: autumn – AE: fall ☐

7 There are different words for the number '0'. Which one is wrong?

a) Yesterday it was five degrees below *zero*. ☐
b) At a tennis match: 15 – 0 (fifteen – *love*) ☐
c) On the phone: 17308 (one – seven – three – *zero* – eight) ☐
d) The game ended 2:0 (two – *nil*) ☐

8 Which of these people is not your relative?

a) brother ☐
b) sister ☐
c) uncle ☐
d) neighbour ☐

9 Kreuze die *falsche* Bedeutung an.

In vielen Actionfilmen werden die gefährlichsten Szenen von einem *Stuntman*, d.h. einem … dargestellt.

a) Ersatzdarsteller ☐
b) Statisten ☐
c) Double ☐
d) Doppelgänger ☐

Language

10 Which word doesn't have a [ð]?

a) the ☐
b) this ☐
c) thank ☐
d) weather ☐

11 **Which word doesn't have a [θ]?**

a) through ☐
b) throw ☐
c) Thursday ☐
d) mother ☐

12 **Which definition is wrong?**

a) XS – extra small ☐
b) S – small ☐
c) M – middle ☐
d) XL – extra large ☐

13 **Complete this proverb.**

When the cat's away, the … will play.

a) children ☐
b) rats ☐
c) hamsters ☐
d) mice ☐

14 **Complete this proverb.**

It takes … to tango.

a) two ☐
b) a pair ☐
c) a couple ☐
d) me and you ☐

Reading

15 **Where can you read this sign?**

a) In a prison. ☐
b) At a four star hotel. ☐
c) At a hospital. ☐
d) At a station. ☐

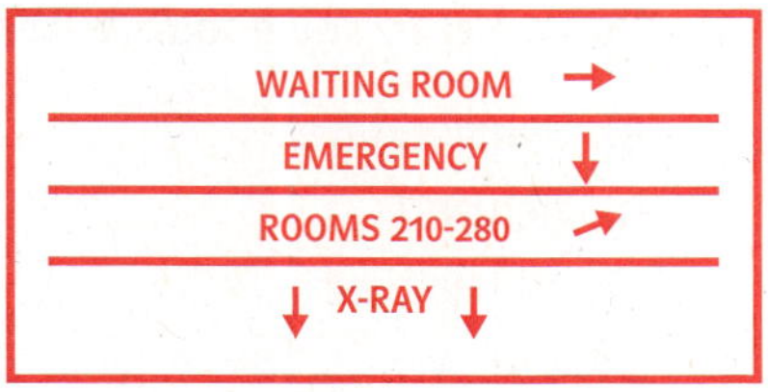

16 **What does this notice mean?**

BREAK GLASS IN CASE OF EMERGENCY

a) If there is an emergency, throw your glass on the floor. ☐
b) If there is an accident, break a window to get out. ☐
c) If there are problems on a flight, break the window to get fresh air. ☐
d) If a kitchen is on fire, throw glasses to warn everybody. ☐

17 **Read this ad and then tick the wrong statement.**

a) TSAW sells tickets for all kinds of concerts. ☐
b) You can call TSAW to get tickets for a sports event. ☐
c) TSAW is more than 25 years old. ☐
d) You cannot use the service in Germany, too. ☐

18 **Find the information which is wrong.**

a) TSAW has got an office in Australia. ☐
b) You can call the offices day and night. ☐
c) TSAW has opened a new office in South Africa. ☐
d) There are two offices in the USA. ☐

TICKET SERVICE AROUND THE WORLD (TSAW)

for 24 hours a day – Los Angeles, New York, London, Hong Kong, Sydney;
More than 25 years of pop, rock and classical concerts, theatre performances, sports events in the United Kingdom, Europe and the rest of the world.
We are the world's number one.
Call us in London on (847) 882 3331 or send your e-mail to: TSAW@serviceline.uk
We will open our next office in Cape Town next year.

Communication

19 ***We're going to eat out this evening.* means ...**

We're going to eat in ... this evening.

a) the open air ☐
b) the moonlight ☐
c) our garden ☐
d) a restaurant ☐

20 ***You want to say goodbye.* What can you not say?**

a) See you later. ☐
b) Hi, there. ☐
c) All the best. ☐
d) Give my regards to your parents. ☐

21 **Which reaction is wrong?**

I don't think brand clothes are important. …

a) I not, too. ☐
b) Don't you really? ☐
c) Nor do I. ☐
d) I don't either. ☐

22 **Sending best wishes or greetings. Spot the unsuitable line.**

a) Just a line to say thanks for the lovely photos. ☐
b) We all send you our love. ☐
c) Sorry to hear you are ill – get well soon. ☐
d) We all wish you good luck in your English test. ☐

Grammar

23 **Spot the correct form.**

a) blow – blue – blown ☐
b) grow – grew – grown ☐
c) throw – through – thrown ☐
d) know – new – known ☐

24 **Which preposition is not correct?**

a) London is famous *for* its sights. ☐
d) Many young tourists are interested *in* the London Eye. ☐
c) Londoners are really proud *on* their city. ☐
d) London is different *from* all other towns in Great Britain. ☐

25 **Which sentence is not correct?**

a) This T-shirt is nice, but I think I'll take that one over there. ☐
b) I've had these jeans for ages, so I really need some new. ☐
c) Which of these shoes do you like? – The black ones. ☐
d) What beautiful handbags! Here's the one I like best. ☐

26 **Spot the wrong form of the adverb.**

a) Those little cakes look *delicious*. ☐
b) The fish and chips smell *fantastic*. ☐
c) Apple-pie with cream – that sounds *great*. ☐
d) The vegetable soup tastes *awfully*. ☐

27 ***The pupils at Thomas Tallis School hope ... a lot of money for children in Africa.***

a) they will collect ☐
b) they do collect ☐
c) they won't collect ☐
d) they collect ☐

28 ***v* or *f*? Find the wrong one.**

a) *Life* in Africa isn't easy. ☐
b) In Kenya last year we saw real *live* lions on our safari. ☐
c) The band from Tanzania gave a *life* concert in Manchester. ☐
d) Does your brother still *live* in South Africa? ☐

29 ***v* or *f*? Find the wrong one.**

a) Bradley *saved* his friend Tom from drowning. ☐
b) He always keeps his diary in a *save* place. ☐
c) Kate is *saving* up for a new and *safe* bike. ☐
d) She is sure it will offer more road *safety* than her old bike. ☐

Culture

30 **California is the US state with two outstanding cities: Los Angeles and San Francisco. Which fact about Los Angeles is not true?**

a) 44 Spanish settlers founded L.A. on September 4, 1781. ☐
b) Los Angeles is part of Hollywood. ☐
c) The Hollywood Walk of Fame shows more than 2,000 stars of famous people. ☐
d) Many stars live in Beverly Hills which is southwest of Hollywood. ☐

31 Which fact about San Francisco is not true?

a) The Golden Gate Bridge is a gateway to San Francisco. ☐
b) Fisherman's Wharf is a place which offers a wonderful view of the Golden Gate Bridge. ☐
c) Old cable cars are a tourist attraction in San Francisco. ☐
d) Alcatraz has long been one of the best hotels in San Francisco. ☐

32 Who is it?

a) Lance Armstrong ☐
b) Michael Jordan ☐
c) Arnold Schwarzenegger ☐
d) Tom Cruise ☐

Born on 30th July 1947 he grew up in Austria. As a young man he was a very successful bodybuilder. Hollywood offered him roles in some exciting action films. A new Hollywood action film star was born. In 1983 he became a U.S. citizen, but he did not give up his Austrian citizenship.
Three years later he married television journalist Maria Shriver. The couple have four children.
He is a Republican and was first elected Governor of California in 2003. He was re-elected and started his a second term on January 5, 2007. He is the 38th Governor of the U.S. State of California.

33 Read the text again and find the wrong statement.

a) As a young man he was a well-known bodybuilder. ☐
b) He became world famous for action films. ☐
c) He is now only a citizen of America. ☐
d) He was elected Govenor of California twice. ☐

34 Which physical exercises to train your body do you not practise in a gym?

a) aerobics ☐
b) diving ☐
c) stretching ☐
d) sit-ups and press-ups ☐

Extra tip

35 Welcher Tipp ist wenig hilfreich, wenn du dein Hörverstehen verbessern willst?

Ich . . . , um mein Hörverstehen zu verbessern.
a) schaue englische Filme an ☐
b) versuche die englischen Texte meiner Lieblings-CDs herauszuhören ☐
c) schalte ab und zu auf BBC World oder CNN im Fernsehen ☐
d) benutze beim Sprechen möglichst oft englische Wörter ☐

Test 1

1 c); 2 b); 3 a); 4 c); 5 c); 6 c) (AE: grade); 7 c); 8 b); 9 c); 10 b); 11 a); 12 b) (a.m. = ante meridiem – vor 12 Uhr Mittag); 13 a) (deutsche Entsprechung: Was Hänschen nicht lernt, lernt Hans nimmermehr.); 14 b) (deutsche Entsprechung: Besser spät als nie.); 15 c); 16 a); 17 c); 18 c); 19 d); 20 c); 21 b); 22 c); 23 d) (break – broke – broken); 24 c); 25 c); 26 d); 27 d); 28 d); 29 b); 30 c); 31 a); 32 d); 33 d); 34 b) (Scotland – Edinburgh); 35 c)

Extra information for 30:

THE SHERIFF OF NOTTINGHAM: According to old stories he was Robin Hood's main enemy.
LITTLE JOHN: He was one of Robin Hood's men: He was very big and strong and so his friends called him Little John as a joke.
FRIAR TUCK: He was one of Robin Hood's companions, a fat and cheerful monk.

Test 2

1 c); 2 b), 3 b); 4 c), 5 d), 6 c) (AE: apartment); 7 b) (one thousand five hundred and *fifty* miles); 8 c); 9 a); 10 b); 11 a); 12 b); 13 d) (deutsche Entsprechung: Morgenstund hat Gold im Mund.); 14 b) (deutsche Entsprechung: Ein Spatz in der Hand ist besser als eine Taube auf dem Dach.); 15 c); 16 c); 17 b); 18 a); 19 c), 20 a); 21 d); 22 a); 23 b) (thin*k*); 24 b); 25 c); 26 b); 27 c); 28 c); 29 a); 30 c); 31 a) (not a dozen, but *dozens* of); 32 d) (Faust ist von Goethe); 33 d); 34 c); 35 d)

Extra information for 30:

HENRY VIII (1491–1547): King of England and Lord of Ireland, later King of Ireland, from 1509 until his death. He married six times. He broke up with the Church of Rome and founded the Church of England. One of his daughters was Elizabeth I (1533–1603), who was Queen of England from 1558 – 1603.
NOEL COWARD (1899–1973): English actor, playwright, and composer of popular music.
WILLIAM SHAKESPEARE: He was baptized 26th April 1564 and he died 23rd April 1616;
BOBBY MOORE: English soccer player born 12th April 1941, won soccer world championship with the English national team in July 1966.

Test 3

1 b); 2 c); 3 a); 4 c); 5 b); 6 d) (AE: downtown); 7 d) (ninety-*ninth*); 8 c); 9 b); 10 b); 11 b); 12 b); 13 b) (deutsche Entsprechung: Man soll das Eisen schmieden, solange es noch heiß ist.); 14 a) (deutsche Entsprechung: Wie man sich bettet, so liegt man.); 15 d); 16 a); 17 c); 18 b); 19 a); 20 b); 21 c); 22 c); 23 c) (win – won – *won*); 24 d) (*Who* did he he meet there?); 25 d); 26 a); 27 b); 28 b); 29 b) (too expensive – zu teuer); 30 c); 31 b); 32 d); 33 d); 34 b) (nursery school teacher); 35 c)

Extra information for 30:

Queen Elizabeth II was born 1926 in London. At the age of 21 she married Lieutenant Sir Philip Mountbatten on 20th November 1947. Her husband had become a British citizen and had changed his name from Schleswig-Holstein-Sonderburg-Glücksburg to Mountbatten. Elizabeth became Queen when her father King George died 6th February 1952. The royal family's name, Windsor, was combined with this name and since 1960 the Queen and her family use the surname Mountbatten-Windsor.
Queen Elizabeth and Prince Philip have four children: Charles (born 1948), Anne (born 1950), Andrew (born 1960) and Edward (born 1964). They celebrated their 60th wedding anniversary in 2007.

Test 4

1 b); 2 d); 3 c); 4 b) (AE: candy); 5 a) (once); 6 b) (daisy – Gänseblümchen, lily – Lilie, rose – Rose); 7 d); 8 b); 9 b); 10 a); 11 c); 12 b); 13 b) (deutsche Entsprechung: Wer zuletzt lacht, lacht am besten.); 14 c) (deutsche Entsprechung: Lachen ist die beste Medizin.); 15 b); 16 c); 17 b); 18 a); 19 b); 20 d); 21 d); 22 c); 23 c) (read – *read* – read); 24 c); 25 b); 26 d); 27 d); 28 d) (than); 29 b) (its food – ihr Fressen); 30 d) (5th November); 31 a); 32 a); 33 b) (only boys); 34 a); 35 b)

Extra information for 32:

Winston Churchill (1874 – 1965): English politician who was Prime Minister of Britain during the Second World War. He made many famous speeches; he is remembered for his great leadership; he was Prime Minister again from 1951 – 1955.
He won the Nobel prize for literature in 1953.
Captain James Cook (1728 – 1779): English explorer of the coasts of Australia and New Zealand; he claimed the east coasts of Australia for Britain; he also discovered several islands in the Pacific including Hawaii, where he was killed.
Nelson Mandela: Born 1918 in South Africa, he became the first black president of the country. Mandela, like Martin Luther King and Malcolm X, is a very important fighter against apartheid. He spent 27 years of his life in prison. In 1993 he received the Nobel peace price, together with De Klerk.

Test 5

1 c); 2 a); 3 c); 4 b); 5 c) (AE: backpack); 6 b); 7 b) (Swiss chocolate); 8 c); 9 d); 10 c); 11 d); 12 b) (United Nations); 13 c) (deutsche Entsprechung: Es ist nicht alles Gold, was glänzt.); 14 b) (deutsche Entsprechung: Auf Regen folgt Sonnenschein.); 15 a); 16 b); 17 b); 18 d); 19 b); 20 b); 21 a); 22 c); 23 d) (buil*d* – built – built); 24 d) (one sheep, two *sheep*); 25 c); 26 b); 27 a); 28 a) (fl*ie*s); 29 c) (taking); 30 a); 31 b); 32 d); 33 b); 34 d); 35 c)

Extra information for 32:

CHARLIE CHAPLIN (1989 – 1977): There are 92 films with Charlie Chaplin. Some famous films: The Gold Rush (1925), City Lights (1931), Modern Times (1936), The Great Dictator (1940), A King in New York (1957); He is buried in Vevey, Switzerland. One of his walking sticks was sold at an auction in London for 47,800 pounds in 2004.
OLEG POPOV: born in 1930, was a famous Russian clown in Moscow State circus.
STAN LAUREL (1890 – 1965) and OLIVER HARDY (1892 – 1957) made many humorous popular films in the 1930s) with the same two central characters, who are known in Germany as *Dick und Doof*. Laurel was the smaller thin man and Hardy was the taller fat one.

Test 6

1 c); 2 b) (doctor – surgery); 3 b) (church – pray); 4 b); 5 d) (AE: to send or mail a letter); 6 b) (It's half past eight.); 7 d) (yen); 8 c) (granny); 9 d); 10 a); 11 c); 12 b) (Mister Smith); 13 b) (deutsche Entsprechung: Man soll nicht alles auf eine Karte setzen.); 14 a) (deutsche Entsprechung: Wie gewonnen, so zerronnen.); 15 c); 16 d); 17 b); 18 c); 19 b); 20 d); 21 c); 22 a); 23 d) (l*ea*ve – left – left); 24 b) (*on* TV); 25 b); 26 d) (hard); 27 b); 28 d) (plan – planned); 29 c) (run – running); 30 d) (Loch Ness is a *lake*); 31 b); 32 d); 33 c); 34 a); 35 d)

Extra information for 32:

E. DOUGLAS HOUGEN (1916 – 1999), from Flint in Michigan, USA, was the inventor of the electric bell. He had about 240 foreign and domestic patents. His words: "You're never too young and never too old to invent". His invented the electric doorbell when he was only 14. This was in northern Saskatchewan. There was no electricity. He used a car battery. It worked fine, but the battery had to be shared with the family car.
THOMAS ALVA EDISON (1847 – 1931) was the inventor of the electric bulb.

Test 7

1 b); 2 d) (cook – kitchen); 3 d); 4 c); 5 b); 6 c) (AE: to call someone); 7 d) (2,50 ml = two point fifty millilitres); 8 a); 9 b); 10 b); 11 c); 12 c); 13 b) (deutsche Entsprechung: Zu Hause ist es am schönsten.); 14 d) (deutsche Entsprechung: Mein Heim ist meine Burg. Oder: Das Haus des Mannes ist sein Schloss.); 15 b); 16 c); 17 d); 18 b); 19 c); 20 c); 21 c); 22 a); 23 a) (ch*oo*se – chose – chosen); 24 b) (a) *at* Spanish, c) *in* the world, d) *in* all photos); 25 b); 26 d) (He *doesn't* want to …); 27 b); 28 d); 29 b); 30 a) (The capital of Wales is Cardiff); 31 b) (Prince Charles was born London.) 32 c); 33 c); 34 c) (Knights fought for *their king* and the *king* gave them *land*.); 35 d)

Extra information for 32:

William the Conquerer (1028 – 1087), Duke of Normandy, King of England (William I): During the Battle of Hastings in 1066 he defeated and killed the last Saxon King of England. The battle took place seven miles from Hastings, in a town called Battle today.
Prince William (born 21 June 1982 in London): He is the elder son of Lady Diana and Prince Charles. His parents got divorced in 1992. His mother died in a car accident in Paris in 1997. William is the second in line (after his father) for the throne of England.
Henry VIII: (Siehe Extra information bei Test 2)

Test 8

1 c); 2 b); 3 d); 4 b); 5 c); 6 a) (AE: pants); 7 b); 8 c); 9 b); 10 b); 11 c); 12 d) (£ = pound); 13 c) (deutsche Entsprechung: Übung macht den Meister.); 14 a) (deutsche Entsprechung: Kleider machen Leute.); 15 a); 16 c); 17 d); 18 b); 19 b); 20 d); 21 a); 22 c); 23 c) (begin – began – begun); 24 d) (at); 25 a); 26 a) (*I'll* stay at home.); 27 c); 28 d) (stupid – more stupid); 29 d); 30 c) (The White House is in Washington, D.C.); 31 d) (in 2001); 32 a); 33 d) (Many of his works *are not photos*, they *look like photographic reproductions*.); 34 d), 35 a);

Extra information for 30:

The Empire State Building is a 102-storey Art Deco skyscraper in New York City. It was completed in 1931 and was the highest building in NYC until the construction of the World Trade Center North Tower on December 23, 1970. After the destruction of the World Trade Center in 2001 it is once again the tallest building in New York.
The Statue of Liberty is a large statue that was presented to the United States by France in 1886. It stands at Liberty Island, New York, as a welcome to all visitors, immigrants and returning Americans.
The Times Square took its name from the newspaper 'The New York Times'. It's the centre of international show business. You can find a lot of theatres and cabarets there. The MTV Studios are there, too.

Extra information for 32:

Keith Haring born near London (1958 – 1990), was an American graffiti artist.
Andy Warhol (1928 – 1987) was an American artist who became a central figure in the movement known as Pop art.
Joseph Beuys, (born in 1921 in Krefeld, † in 1986 in Düsseldorf), German artist, sculptor, draughtsman, art theoretician, politician and teacher.

Test 9

1 c); 2 b) (vet – doctor for animals); 3 a) (roadie); 4 b); 5 c); 6 a) (AE: highway); 7 d); 8 b); 9 a); 10 a); 11 c); 12 a) (1 pint = 0.568 litre, 1 ounce is 28,35 grams, 1 pound [= 16 ounces] = 0,4536 kg); 13 d) (deutsche Entsprechung: Schlafende Hunde soll man nicht wecken.); 14 b) (deutsche Entsprechung: Hunde, die bellen, beißen nicht.); 15 c); 16 d); 17 b); 18 d) (a short book is a booklet); 19 a); 20 b); 21 c); 22 d); 23 a) (teach – taught – taught); 24 b) (a) *at*, c) *by*, d) *about*); 25 d); 26 b); 27 d); 28 b) (the eastern states of the USA – kein Eigenname); 29 c) (Queen Elizabeth); 30 b); 31 a) (It's Tallahassee); 32 c); 33 a); 34 c) (The film "Jaws" from 1975 is a thriller directed by Steven Spielberg. It was based on Peter Benchley's best-selling novel which was inspired by the Jersey Shore shark attacks of 1916.); 35 a);

Extra information for 32:

Iwao Takamoto (1925 – 2007) was a Japanese American animator, television producer and film director. He became most famous for producing and designing Scooby-Doo.
Charles Monroe Schulz (1922 – 2000) was a 20th-century American cartoonist. He is best known worldwide for his Peanuts comic strip with its characters Charles, Lucy, Linus and Snoopy.
Matthew Groening born February 15, 1954 in Portland, Oregon; is an Emmy Award-winning American cartoonist and the creator of The Simpsons.

Test 10

1 d); 2 c) (greengrocer – vegetables); 3 d); 4 b) (peregrine falcon: 200.00 miles per hour = mph; antelope: 61.00 mph; lion: 50.00 mph; horse: 47.50 mph; cat: 30.00 mph; human: 27.89 mph; garden snail: 0.03 mph); 5 a) (dairy – Molkerei); 6 a) (AE: wallet); 7 c) (bei Telfonnummern wird die Null wie der Buchstabe '0' ausgesprochen, geschrieben: oh.); 8 d); 9 b); 10 c); 11 d); 12 c) (M = medium); 13 d) (deutsche Entsprechung: Ist die Katze aus dem Haus, tanzen die Mäuse auf dem Tisch.); 14 a) (deutsche Entsprechung: Es gehören immer zwei dazu.); 15 c); 16 b); 17 d); 18 c) (TSAW *will open* a new office in South Africa, Cape Town); 19 d); 20 b); 21 a); 22 a); 23 b) (blow – *blew* – blown, throw – *threw* thrown, know – *knew* – known); 24 c) (proud *of*); 25 b) (… I really need some new *ones*.); 26 d) (nach Verben der Wahrnehmung (look, taste, smell, sound, etc.) kein -ly); 27 a); 28 c); 29 b), 30 b) (umgekehrt: Hollywood is a district of Los Angeles); 31 d) (Alcatraz was a prison); 32 c); 33 c) (He is American *and* Austrian citizen.); 34 b); 35 d)

Extra information for 33:

Lance Armstrong (born 1971) is a retired American professional road racing cyclist. He won the Tour de France seven times, from 1999 to 2005.
Michael Jordan (born 1963 in Brooklyn, NY) is a famous US basketball player; He ended his career at the age of 40 in 2003.
Tom Cruise (born 1962), is an American actor and film producer; Some of his films are Top Gun (1986), Rain Man (1988) The Firm (1993), Mission: Impossible (1996); Vanilla Sky (2001); Valkyrie (2008).

Your test report

Tip 1: Always mark your answers with a pencil so that you can do the tasks again.
Tip 2: Check your answers on page 74–79.
Tip 3: Count your right answers and make a cross in the table below.
Tip 4: Read the comment on your result on the next page.

right answers:	**31–35**	**28–30**	**22–27**	**17–21**	**9–16**	**0–8**
Test 1						
Test 2						
Test 3						
Test 4						
Test 5						
Test 6						
Test 7						
Test 8						
Test 9						
Test 10						

Comment on your test result

31–35 right answers:	**Excellent!**	You did very well! Go on to the next test.
28–30 right answers:	**Very good!**	Erase your crosses or ticks and do the wrong tasks again. Then check your answers again.
22–27 right answers:	**Not bad!**	Mark your wrong answers with a coloured pencil. Do these tasks again after two or three days. Look up the difficult words in a dictionary.
17–21 right answers:	**Satisfactory!**	Look at all the wrong tasks again. Do ten of these tasks the next day, repeat until all answers are correct. Look up the difficult words in a dictionary. Do some grammar revision.
9–16 right answers:	**You can do better!**	Think positive, but you have to do more to get a better mark. Read as much English as you can and learn some English words every day. Write ten words on cards every day and learn them. Do more grammar revision.
0–8 right answers:	**No comment!**	Are you sure that you tried hard?